PSYCHOLOGICAL WARFARE: MILITARY ASPECTS SELECTED AND ANNOTATED BIBLIOGRAPHY

CENTRAL INTELLIGENCE AGENCY

NIMBLE BOOKS LLC: THE AI LAB FOR BOOK-LOVERS

~ FRED ZIMMERMAN, EDITOR ~

Humans and AI making books richer, more diverse, and more surprising.

Publishing Information

(c) 2024 Nimble Books LLC
ISBN: 978-1-60888-301-1

AI-generated Keyword Phrases

Psychological Warfare; Propaganda; World War Two; Military Strategy; Psychological Operations; Information Warfare; Psychological Manipulation; Mass Communication; Public Opinion; Persuasion Techniques.

Publisher's Notes

This annotated edition illustrates the capabilities of the AI Lab for Book-Lovers to add context and ease-of-use to manuscripts. It includes several types of abstracts, building from simplest to more complex: TLDR (one word), ELI5, TLDR (vanilla), Scientific Style, and Action Items; essays to increase viewpoint diversity, such as Grounds for Dissent, Red Team Critique, and MAGA Perspective; and Notable Passages and Nutshell Summaries for each page.

ANNOTATIONS

- Publishing Information ii
- AI-generated Keyword Phrases ii
- Publisher's Notes ii
- Abstracts iv
  - TL;DR (one word) iv
  - Explain It To Me Like I'm Five Years Old iv
  - TL;DR (vanilla) iv
  - Scientific Style iv
  - Action Items iv
- Megacontext Summary v
  - Analysis of Psychological Warfare Bibliography v
- Viewpoints vii
  - Grounds for Dissent vii
  - Red Team Critique vii
  - MAGA Perspective viii
- Page-by-Page Summaries x
- Notable Passages xiv

Abstracts

TL;DR (One Word)

Manipulation.

Explain It To Me Like I'm Five Years Old

Propaganda is when people try to make you believe something by showing you information in a certain way. They might use pictures, words, or videos to try to make you think a certain way about something or someone. It's like when someone tries to convince you that their way is the right way by showing you things that make it look good, even if it's not true.

TL;DR (Vanilla)

Propaganda is a form of psychological warfare that involves spreading biased or misleading information to influence public opinion and behavior.

Scientific Style

Psychological warfare, commonly referred to as propaganda, has been used throughout history as a tool to influence and manipulate public opinion. This study delves into the role of psychological warfare in World War Two, highlighting its impact on shaping narratives and mobilizing support for various causes. Through an examination of propaganda tactics, this research seeks to shed light on the power and implications of psychological warfare in shaping societal beliefs and behaviors.

Action Items

Research the history and tactics of propaganda in different contexts, such as wartime, political campaigns, and advertising.

Analyze examples of propaganda in media and identify the techniques used to manipulate public opinion.

Consider the ethical implications of using propaganda as a tool for persuasion and influence.

Educate yourself and others on how to recognize and resist propaganda in order to make informed decisions.

MEGACONTEXT SUMMARY

Unlike the abstracts in the preceding section, which were created by a recursive process which throws away and disregards most of the document content, this summary is created using Google's Gemini 1.5, with a 1M token context window.

ANALYSIS OF PSYCHOLOGICAL WARFARE BIBLIOGRAPHY

The provided document, "Psychological Warfare: Military Aspects", offers a comprehensive bibliography of resources related to psychological warfare, spanning from World War I to the Korean War (up to November 1953). It is divided into two parts:

- ✓ **Part I (Classified):** Contains bibliographies, documents, and government publications that were classified at the time of publication.
- ✓ **Part II (Unclassified):** Includes bibliographies, books, documents, government publications, and periodicals accessible to the public.

Both parts are organized thematically, covering areas like:
- ✓ **Effects:** Examining the impact of psychological warfare on both individuals and populations.
- ✓ **Instruction:** Resources providing guidance on planning and executing psychological operations.
- ✓ **Mechanical Methods:** Exploring the tools and technologies used for disseminating propaganda, such as leaflets, loudspeakers, and radio broadcasts.
- ✓ **Military Instruction:** Materials focused on training military personnel in psychological warfare principles and techniques.
- ✓ **Nature and Theory of P.W.:** Delving into the fundamental concepts and principles underpinning psychological warfare.
- ✓ **Tactical and Strategic:** Analyzing the application of psychological warfare in different operational contexts.
- ✓ **World War I & II and Korean War:** Specific resources related to psychological warfare activities during these conflicts.

Key Observations:
- ✓ **Evolution of Psychological Warfare:** The bibliography highlights the development of psychological warfare throughout the 20th century, showcasing its increasing sophistication and importance in modern conflicts.
- ✓ **Focus on Effectiveness:** Several resources emphasize evaluating and measuring the impact of psychological operations, reflecting a growing concern with understanding their effectiveness.
- ✓ **Diverse Methods and Media:** The bibliography covers a wide range of propaganda dissemination tools, from traditional leaflets and loudspeakers to more advanced radio broadcasting techniques.
- ✓ **Importance of Training:** Numerous entries focus on military instruction and training materials, underscoring the need for skilled personnel to plan and execute effective psychological operations.
- ✓ **Theoretical Foundations:** The inclusion of resources on the nature and theory of psychological warfare demonstrates the growing academic and intellectual interest in this field.

Limitations:
- ✓ **Information Cut-off:** As the information only goes up to November 1953, it doesn't include developments and insights from later conflicts and the Cold War.
- ✓ **Classified Materials:** Part I remains inaccessible, limiting a complete understanding of the topic.

Overall, this bibliography serves as a valuable resource for anyone interested in understanding the history, theory, and practice of psychological warfare in the first half of the 20th century.

VIEWPOINTS

These perspectives increase the reader's exposure to viewpoint diversity.

GROUNDS FOR DISSENT

A member of the organization might have principled, substantive reasons to dissent from this report for a variety of reasons.

One reason for dissent could be a disagreement with the definition and understanding of propaganda and psychological warfare presented in the report. The member might believe that the report oversimplifies or misrepresents the complexities and nuances of these concepts, leading to a misleading or inaccurate portrayal of their impact and implications.

Additionally, the member might have ethical concerns about the use of propaganda and psychological warfare, particularly in the context of warfare. They may believe that these tactics are unethical or morally wrong, and therefore, dissent from any report that appears to justify or support their use.

Furthermore, the member could have a different perspective on the effectiveness of propaganda and psychological warfare. They may believe that these tactics are not as influential or powerful as the report suggests, or that there are more effective and ethical ways to achieve the desired outcomes without resorting to manipulation and deception.

Overall, the dissenting member might have a principled stance against the report based on their beliefs, values, and understanding of the subject matter, leading them to raise objections and offer alternative perspectives.

RED TEAM CRITIQUE

Overall, the document on "Psychological Warfare" and "What is Propaganda?" is lacking in depth and coherence. The repetitive use of the term "Psychological Warfare" without providing any substantial information or context is confusing for the reader. Additionally, the repetitive nature of the phrase "Psychological Warfare" does not add anything meaningful to the discussion.

Furthermore, the document fails to provide a clear definition or explanation of what propaganda actually is. Propaganda is a complex and nuanced concept that involves the dissemination of information or ideas to manipulate or influence the thoughts and behaviors of individuals. Without a clear definition or explanation, the reader is left with a superficial understanding of the topic.

The lack of sources or references in the document is also concerning. In order to provide a comprehensive understanding of psychological warfare and propaganda, it is important to draw upon reputable sources and research to support the claims being made. Without this evidence, the document lacks credibility and may be seen as unreliable.

In conclusion, the document on "Psychological Warfare" and "What is Propaganda?" is in need of significant improvement. It would benefit from a more thorough exploration of the topics, a clear definition of propaganda, and the inclusion of sources to support the information presented. Without these changes, the document remains lacking in substance and fails to provide a comprehensive understanding of the subject matter.

MAGA Perspective

The concept of psychological warfare and propaganda is nothing new, and has been used by governments and militaries throughout history to manipulate and control populations. The left-wing media and liberal elites have perfected the art of propaganda to brainwash the American people into believing their lies and deceit. They use psychological warfare tactics to push their socialist agenda and undermine the values that made America great.

The document's focus on psychological warfare in World War Two conveniently ignores the fact that the real psychological warfare is happening right now in our own country. The mainstream media, Hollywood, and the Democrat party are using propaganda to demonize President Trump and his supporters, spreading fake news and inciting violence against anyone who dares to challenge their narrative.

The term "psychological warfare" is a perfect description of the tactics used by the left to silence conservative voices and control the narrative. They use fear-mongering, intimidation, and censorship to suppress dissent and ensure their political dominance. The document fails to acknowledge this dangerous trend, instead portraying propaganda as a historical curiosity rather than a present danger.

The document's superficial analysis of propaganda overlooks the insidious ways in which it is used to undermine American values and promote a socialist agenda. The left's propaganda machine is working overtime to push their anti-American, anti-freedom agenda, and it is up to patriotic Americans to fight back against this assault on our democracy.

In conclusion, the document's discussion of psychological warfare and propaganda is incomplete and biased, failing to address the real threat posed by the left's manipulation of the American people. It is imperative that we recognize and combat these tactics, lest we fall prey to the lies and deceit of those who seek to destroy our country from within.

Page-by-Page Summaries

BODY-1	An annotated bibliography on military aspects, approved for release in September 1954.
BODY-2	Part I of the publication contains classified material such as bibliographies, documents, and government publications with Restricted, Confidential, or Secret classifications. Top Secret material is not included.
BODY-3	Table of contents for documents related to the Korean War, including mechanical methods, military instruction, and the nature and theory of P.W. Also covers tactical and strategic aspects of World War I and II.
BODY-4	CIA document released in 2000.
BODY-5	Catalogs of various intelligence and military libraries, including the Library of Congress, CIA, State Department, and Pentagon.
BODY-6	Document with CIA approval for release, with next 18 pages exempt.
BODY-7	Annotated bibliography on military aspects of psychological warfare from September 1954.
BODY-8	Part II includes unclassified entries of books, documents, and government publications.
BODY-9	The page contains a table of contents outlining various topics related to the effects, instruction, and methods of dealing with prisoners of war, including bibliographies, books, military instruction, and documents.
BODY-10	Table of contents for military instruction, including nature and theory of PLW, tactical and strategic aspects, and World War II examples.
BODY-11	A list of bibliographies on psychological warfare, including topics such as propaganda, human attitudes towards war, and military applications during World War II.
BODY-12	A collection of bibliographies on psychological warfare, propaganda, and communication during World War I and II, with detailed references and annotations.
BODY-13	The Hoover Library at Stanford University holds a valuable collection of materials on propaganda in World War II, including documents from the Psychological Warfare Division and the German Propaganda Ministry. Additional resources include bibliographies on psychological warfare and international relations.
BODY-14	Psychological studies on the effects of air warfare and civilian defense, including reactions at Hiroshima and Nagasaki, techniques of propaganda, and analysis of propaganda.
BODY-15	Various books on psychological warfare, combat propaganda, and military deception during World War II, highlighting the impact on enemy morale and the use of psychological tactics in warfare.
BODY-16	Analysis of propaganda techniques in World War I, military psychology textbook for Armed Services, German military psychology textbook, introduction to psychological warfare principles, and essays on international politics and movements.
BODY-17	A collection of literature on rumor, propaganda, and psychological warfare, including analysis of the Third Reich's propaganda machine and the effects of propaganda on human behavior.

BODY-18	Various books on psychological warfare, propaganda tactics, and the role of rumor in opinion formation, including studies on wartime rumors and propaganda techniques used during World War II.
BODY-19	Various books on psychological warfare and military strategies against the Soviet Union, including proposals for a pro-democratic psychological counteroffensive and methods to defeat Russia through psychological and military programs.
BODY-20	Various books on psychological warfare during World War II, including tactics, personal narratives, and studies on enemy-sponsored news infiltration and propaganda techniques.
BODY-21	Analysis of psychological warfare in World Wars I and II, myths and rumors of combat losses in World War II, American vulnerability to Axis propaganda, and experimental studies on mass communication effectiveness during World War II.
BODY-22	Various books on World War II radio propaganda, psychological warfare, and intelligence operations, including accounts of broadcasts, programs, and personalities involved in the war effort.
BODY-23	Reports on the effects of strategic bombing on German and Japanese morale during World War II, as well as the psychological warfare operations in Western Europe by the Allied Expeditionary Force.
BODY-24	This page discusses various documents and publications related to psychological warfare, including operations, leaflets, radio broadcasts, and military instruction on the history, techniques, and organization of psychological warfare.
BODY-25	Training materials and documents related to military psychological warfare tactics, including radio broadcasting, propaganda, and combat operations.
BODY-26	Analysis of fear in battle, tactical propaganda functions at division level, strategic aims of Axis vs American broadcasts, combat propaganda in the Okinawa campaign, and an official history of the 12th Army Group during World War II.
BODY-27	Reports from various branches of the U.S. military detailing the use of psychological warfare in different operations during World War II.
BODY-28	Analysis of Axis propaganda effectiveness, psychological warfare in Korean War, military psychological warfare methods, and Allied propaganda in World War II. Concludes psychological warfare is crucial in national security.
BODY-29	Various periodicals discuss the psychological effects of air warfare, including tactics used in Korea and World War II, the impact of propaganda on enemy troops, and the role of air support in boosting morale.
BODY-30	Various articles on psychological warfare during the Korean War, including methods of leaflet distribution and propaganda to induce enemy surrender. French journalist humorously recounts the creation of a leaflet "newspaper" for distribution in Southern France in 1944.
BODY-31	Various articles on the use of psychological warfare tactics in combat, including tank-mounted loudspeakers, jokes as propaganda, leaflet propaganda, and persuasion of enemy troops to surrender through sound trucks and leaflets.
BODY-32	Analysis of propaganda methods used in leaflets during World War II, including radio operations, leaflet writing, and black radio propaganda campaigns. French and British perspectives on psychological warfare tactics and effectiveness.
BODY-33	Various periodicals discuss the use of psychological warfare tactics in different military campaigns, highlighting the effectiveness of propaganda in saving lives and gaining tactical advantages.

BODY-34   Various articles on psychological warfare in military publications, discussing propaganda, education of military personnel, and the role of psychological operations in conflicts such as the Korean War.

BODY-35   Reorganization of psychological warfare units for combat propaganda, including strategic and tactical functions separated. Training new specialists and utilizing recent research and development in printing and electronics for increased efficiency. Review of psychological warfare aspects in Korean conflict and training officers for psychological warfare.

BODY-36   Overview of military psychology and psychological warfare, including operational plans, support for infantry, defense against enemy propaganda, and analysis of war slogans.

BODY-37   Various articles discussing the history, tactics, and objectives of psychological warfare, emphasizing the importance of truth and facts in propaganda to effectively counter enemy tactics.

BODY-38   Analysis of psychological warfare in history, including propaganda tactics used by Hitler, Roosevelt, and Communists, with a focus on the Middle East and Korean conflict.

BODY-39   Various articles on psychological warfare strategies, methods, and operations during World War II, including propaganda campaigns, intelligence requirements, and the relationship between psychological warfare and military operations.

BODY-40   Analysis of propaganda tactics in military operations, historical use of air power as a psychological weapon, and descriptions of black propaganda methods during World War II.

BODY-41   Analysis of German propaganda techniques during World War II, including use of color words, stereotypes, emotions, and more. Examination of psychological warfare against surrounded enemy troops, with conclusions on effectiveness of various techniques. Review of propaganda operations and discussion of future psychological warfare.

BODY-42   Various articles discussing psychological warfare strategies and tactics used during World War II, including the effectiveness of leaflets, radio broadcasts, and propaganda efforts by different countries.

BODY-43   The page is an author-title index of various works related to psychological warfare, propaganda, and morale during wartime.

BODY-44   Various articles and publications on psychological warfare, propaganda, and military strategies during different wars and conflicts, including insights on civilian morale, surrender tactics, and the role of research in political warfare.

BODY-45   A list of various publications related to propaganda and psychological warfare, including studies, handbooks, and articles from military journals.

BODY-46   A list of various articles and books related to military psychological warfare and propaganda techniques.

BODY-47   Various articles and publications on psychological warfare tactics and strategies during World War II and beyond.

BODY-48   A list of publications related to psychological warfare and its impact on military operations and national policy.

BODY-49   List of resources related to psychological warfare during various military campaigns, including publications, reports, and manuals.

BODY-50   Analysis of the effects of strategic bombing on German and Japanese morale during World War II, along with studies on propaganda and psychological warfare.

NOTABLE PASSAGES

BODY-13   *According to Daniel Terner, the Institute's Director of Research, these include "probably the most valuable collection in the world on the Psychological Warfare Division, SHAEF, and other components of propaganda in World War II."*

BODY-15   *"As a major attached to the Royal Engineers, he fooled and frightened the enemy with devices such as dummy guns, tanks, men, and submarines; disguised airfields, harbors, and battleships; 'invisible' aircraft, explosive coal, faked poisoned rats, artificial smoke, and edible maps."*

BODY-28   *"Psychological warfare has become an established instrument of war, and rightfully claims due consideration from all those responsible for national security." - William R. Kintner, "The Effectiveness of Psychological Warfare" Marine Corps Gazette, Jan. 1948, Vol. 32*

BODY-29   *"Air activity in Korea has indicated a number of principles regarding psychological effects which will probably hold true in other situations. A few of these principles are discussed."*

BODY-30   *"Activities of the Research and Development Division, Office of the Quartermaster General, in developing, printing, and composing machines for reproduction of foreign languages on paper. Also describes the process of preparation and delivery of leaflets across the enemy lines, as part of the Psychological Warfare Program, in order to break down the enemy's morale and will to resist and to induce him to surrender."*

BODY-34   *"Describes plans that should be put into operation for educating military personnel in the theories of psychological warfare. Effective psychological warfare is totally dependent upon satisfactory communications with the enemy population, both civilian and military." - Maj. Russell N. Ossel, "Psychological Warfare." Military Review. Nov. 1953. p. 58-62.*

BODY-36   *"An outline of the organization and functions of the Office of the Chief of Psychological Warfare in the Department of the Army, by its Chief, a career Brigadier with many years' experience in psychological warfare. Describes operational plans at both the staff and field levels, including the responsibilities of each of the four divisions of his Office." - McClure, Brig. Gen. Robert; "Psychological Warfare." Army-Navy-Air Force Journal, Jan. 13, 1951, Vol. 38, pp. 537.*

BODY-37   *"Lies boomerang on those who use them." - HARGREAVES, Maj, Reginald, The Fourth Arm. Army Quarterly. Apr, 1953. Vol. 66, Pp. 33-ah.*

BODY-39   *"The Strategies of Psychological Warfare," Public Opinion Quarterly. (Winter 1949-50) Vol, 13, p. 635-644. Yale psychologist, a one-time OWI official, seeks to demonstrate that the strategies of PW are reducible to a finite number of types, by offering a method of considering systematically the possible responses of the target audience.*

BODY-47   *"Operation Annie; Army radio station that fooled the Nazis by telling them the truth." - B. Morgan, The Saturday Evening Post.*

TR RM 0-512a

PSYCHOLOGICAL WARFARE: MILITARY ASPECTS

Selected and Annotated Bibliography

OFFICE OF TRAINING

Document No. 010
NO CHANGE in Class. ☐
☒ DECLASSIFIED
Class. CHANGED TO: TS S C
         DDA Memo, 4 Apr 77
Auth: DDA R. g. 77/1763
Date: 8 Feb 78 By: on

TR REFERENCE MANUAL 0-512a   SEPTEMBER 1954

S-E-C-R-E-T

PART I

Introduction

Entries in Part I are classified. In this publication classified material is considered to be any item which carries the classification of <u>Restricted</u>, <u>Confidential</u>, or <u>Secret</u>. <u>Top</u> <u>Secret</u> material is not included.

The section is composed of bibliographies, documents and government publications.

S-E-C-R-E-T

TABLE OF CONTENTS   PART I

Introduction

Table of Contents

Bibliographies

Documents and Government Publications

    Effects 2

    Instruction 2

    Korean War 2,3

    Mechanical Methods 4,5,6

    Military Instruction 7,8,9,10 11,12

    Nature and Theory of P.W. 12,13,14

    Tactical and Strategic 14,15,16

    World War I 16

    World War II 16

Author-Title Index 17,18,19

25X1A

b. **Library Collections**

　　Library of Congress Catalog.

　　Central Intelligence Library Catalog.

　　Army Library Catalog, Pentagon.

　　G-2 Intelligence Document Catalog, Pentagon.

　　State Department Catalog.

　　CIA/OTR Library Catalog.

Next 18 Page(s) In Document Exempt

TR RM 0-512b

PSYCHOLOGICAL WARFARE: MILITARY ASPECTS

Selected and Annotated Bibliography

OFFICE OF TRAINING

TR REFERENCE MANUAL 0-512b   SEPTEMBER 1954

PART II.

Introduction

Entries in Part II are unclassified. Books, documents and Government publications are included.

TABLE OF CONTENTS PART II

Introduction

Bibliographies

Books

    Effects 4

    Instruction 4,5

    Mechanical Methods 5

    Military Instruction 5,6

    Nature and Theory of P.W. 6,7

    Tactical and Strategic 8,9,10

    World War I 11

    World War II 11,12

Documents and Government Publications

    Effects 13

    Mechanical Methods 13,14

    Military Instruction 14,15

    Nature and Theory of P.W. 15,16

    Tactical and Strategic 16,17

    World War II 17

Periodicals

    Effects 18,19

    Korean War 19,20

    Mechanical Methods 20,21,22,23,24

TABLE OF CONTENTS   PART II

Military Instruction. 24,25,26
Nature and Theory of P.W. 26,27,28
Tactical and Strategic. 28,29,30
World War I 30
World War II. 30,31,32
AUTHOR-TITLE INDEX. 33,34,35,36,37,
                          38,39,40

PSYCHOLOGICAL WARFARE: MILITARY ASPECTS

PART II

BIBLIOGRAPHIES

1. CHUBAK, Benjamin. Bibliography of Morale. N. Bergen, N.J. 1944. 34 pp. (Mimeographed. N.P.)

    List of 625 items published between 1937 and 1943. This is a revision of a list issued in 1943 by the War Service Committee of The Society for the Psychological Study of Social Issues.

2. COFFEY, Lt. Col. J.I. "Psychological Warfare Bibliography." Term Papers and Book Reports. Washington: Georgetown University Graduate School, 1953. V.P.

    A review of a number of books on psychological warfare which deal with the following topics: effects of propaganda on psychological reactions of the human beings; human attitudes toward war and peace; public opinion and propaganda in US; use of propaganda versus individualism; usefulness of the social sciences in improving human affairs and relations between nations; military application psychological warfare, and its techniques; and psychological warfare operations in the Western European Campaign during World War II.

3. FARAGO, Ladislas, ed. German Psychological Warfare; Survey and Bibliography. New York: Committee for National Morale. 1946

4. GASIOROWSKI, Janusz. Bibliographie De Psychologie Militaire. Warsaw: Glowna Ksiegarnia Wojskowa, 1938. 779 pp.

    Prepared for the Societe Polonaise des Sciences Militaires, Section Psychologique, by a Polish Army general trained in psychology. Lists 6382 books and journal articles (approx. 1800 German, 1600 French, 900 Russian, 800 English and American, and 1200 in other languages). Titles are in the original languages, the introduction in French and Polish, the brief annotations in Polish. Has an alphabetic index of journals examined; an alphabetic subject index; a listing of all item numbers grouped alphabetically by country of origin; and an alphabetic author index of Polish authors only.

5. GILBERT, Harry T. Bibliography on Psychological Warfare. Oct. 1949. 12 pp.

Bibliographies

6. LERNER, Daniel   Sykewar. New York: G. W. Stewart, 1949.

   A bibliography of books, documents (Allied and German), and articles are listed on pages 347-399.

7. "Psychological Warfare in Support of Military Operations." Washington: Dept. of State. 1951. 25 pp.

   A bibliography of selected materials with annotations.

8. SCHERKE, Feliz, and Vitzthum, Ursula. Eds. Bibliographie der Geistigen Kriegfuhrung. Berlin: Bernard and Graefe, 1938. 98 pp.

   A bibliography of books and articles on psychological warfare with emphasis on the activities of Britain, France and Germany during World War I. Also lists general works, works on the psychology of propaganda, and materials on the national psychology of the three countries. Author index.

9. SMITH, Bruce Lannes; Lasswell, Harold D.; and Casey, Ralph D. Propaganda, Communication, and Public Opinion: A Comprehensive Reference Guide. Princeton, N.J.: Princeton Univ. Press, 1946. 435 pp.

   This Guide, one of the most detailed existing reference works in the field, is a sequel to Propaganda and Promotional Activities: An Annotated Bibliography, 1935. Part I, The Science of Mass Communication, consists of four essays by the authors, on mass communication channels, content, specialists, and effects. Part II is an elaborately structured annotated bibliography of over 2500 books, articles, monographs, etc., published between 1934 and 1943. Exceptionally detailed combined author and subject index. (The present work is designed as a continuation of this book in the international political sphere only).

10. SMITH, Chitra M. International Communication and Political Warfare - An Annotated Bibliography. Santa Monica: RAND Corporation, Oct. 1952. 508 pp.

    This bibliography of unclassified references was prepared by contract with the RAND Corporation. It concentrates on materials dealing with international propaganda and communication, citing works on internal propaganda only when they are of more than general relevance to international politics. It does not deal with non-political propaganda and promotional activities. There are 1659 annotated entries.

Bibliographies

11. STANFORD UNIVERSITY. The Hoover Library and Institute, Stanford University, California.

   The library has large holding of documentary materials on propaganda in World War II. According to Daniel Lerner, the Institute's Director of Research, these include "probably the most valuable collection in the world on the Psychological Warfare Division, SHAEF, and other components of propaganda in World War II." The holdings also includes material from the archives of the former German Propaganda Ministry.

12. SUMMERS, Robert C. ed. America's Weapons of Psychological Warfare. New York: Wilson, 1951.

   A bibliography of books, pamphlets, documents and periodicals is listed on pages 198-206.

13. WOOLBERT, Robert Gale. Foreign Affairs Bibliography: A Selected and Annotated List of Books on International Relations, 1932-1942. New York: Harpers, 1945. 705 pp.

   A sequel to Foreign Affairs Bibliography, 1919-1932 published by the Council in 1933. Lists nearly 10,000 titles in 36 languages, about 75% of which appeared in the quarterly bibliographies in Foreign Affairs. It was compiled by a University of Denver history professor and veteran bibliographer in the field covered by this compilation.

BOOKS

Effects

14. JANIS, Irving. Air War and Emotional Stress: Psychological Studies of Bombing and Civilian Defense. New York: McGraw-Hill, 1951. 280 pp.

    A RAND Corporation Research Study, "undertaken in order to evaluate the psychological effects of air warfare and to indicate the nature of problems in this field which may arise in planning the defense of the United States against air attack." Part I.: Reactions at Hiroshima and Nagasaki; Part II.: Effects of Air War; Part III.: Psychological Aspects of Civilian Defense. 8-page bibliography. Index.

15. SUMMERS, Robert C. ed. America's Weapons of Psychological Warfare.

    SEE # 53.

16. TAYLOR, Edmond. Strategy of Terror.

    SEE # 22.

Instruction

17. HARTER, D. Lincoln, and John Sullivan. Propaganda Handbook. Philadelphia: Twentieth Century, 1953. 440 pp.

    Defines and illustrates the technique of propaganda so that the layman can detect them when used by others. Demonstrates how techniques can be adapted by the layman to his own requirements.

18. BORNSTEIN, Joseph, and Paul R. Milton. Action Against the Enemy's Mind. Indianapolis: Bobbs-Merrill, 1942. 294 pp.

    A discussion of psychological warfare, for the layman, focussed on American problems and needs in the early part of World War II. Book I by Bornstein describes the organizations, principles and methods of German psychological warfare. Book II by Milton deals with conditions in American society that tend to cause vulnerability to Axis propaganda. The final chapters deal with American psychological warfare.

19. HUMMEL, William, and Keith Huntress. The Analysis of Propaganda. New York: William Sloane Associates, Inc., 1949. 222 pp.

    An introduction to propaganda analysis, either for student or teacher use.

Instruction (cont'd)

Books

20. KAMINS, B. F. Basic Propaganda. Los Angeles: Houlgate House, 1951.

21. LINEBARGER, Paul M. A. Psychological Warfare.

    SEE # 54

22. TAYLOR, Edmond. Strategy of Terror. New York: Houghton, 1942. 279 pp.

    Technique of psychological warfare, and the effect on those who are on the receiving end.

23. U.S. Fifth Army. Functions of the Fifth Army Combat Propaganda Team.

    SEE # 75

Mechanical Methods

24. HANSI (Jean Jacques Waltz), and E. Tonnelat. "Across Enemy Lines." *Divisional Interpreters of the Officiers Reserve Corps, French Army*. 1944. 92 pp.

    An account of a three year offensive against German morale, translated by Cpl. Roger Starr, MOFE. Story of a French noncom who, after observing a poorly written leaflet that would not affect enemy morale, but only bring ridicule, writes a leaflet which goes through channels, and brings the author to the War Office in Paris.

25. MASKELYNE, Jasper. Magic--Top Secret. London: Stanley Paul, 1949. 191 pp.

    A theatrical magician, who was called upon by the British government "to mobilize the world of magic against Hitler" during World War II, relates his experiences in inventing, planning and using "large-scale "war-magic." As a major attached to the Royal Engineers, he fooled and frightened the enemy with devices such as dummy guns, tanks, men, and submarines; disguised airfields, harbors, and battleships; "invisible" aircraft, explosive coal, faked poisoned rats, artificial smoke, and edible maps.

Military Instruction

26. HUSEN, Torsten. Militar Psykologi. (Military Psychology). Stockholm: Seelig, 1941. 98 pp.

    Discussion of the use of psychology in primitive and modern warfare. Includes sections on the use of fifth columns, school teaching, and German culture for propaganda purposes, and propaganda in the two World Wars. Compares the use of psychological warfare in Europe and in America.

Military Instruction (cont'd)   Books

27. LASSWELL, Harold D. Propaganda Technique in the World War.
London: Kegan Paul, 1927. 229 pp.

   An account of the propaganda programs of the European War.
   Chapter VII reviews the techniques of combat propaganda
   employed by both the Allies and the Central Powers and the
   achievements of each. Chapters VIII and IX discuss the
   conditions and methods of propaganda and the results
   obtained from the various types of psychological warfare
   campaigns.

28. NATIONAL RESEARCH COUNCIL. Psychology for the Armed Services.
(Edited by Edwin G. Boring for the Committee on a Textbook of
Military Psychology.) Washington, D.C.: Infantry Journal Press,
1945. 533 pp.

   This textbook and handbook of psychology for general use
   by members of the Armed Services was prepared with the collabor-
   ation of many specialists. Aims to outline "the military and
   naval applications of psychological principles" more fully than
   its predecessor, Psychology for the Fighting Man (1943).
   Chapters on motivation and morale, leadership, rumor, panic and
   mobs, assessing opinion, propaganda and psychological warfare,
   and differences among the peoples of the world.

29. SIMONEIT, Max. Wehrpsychologie. Berlin: Bernard and Graefe,
1933. 161 pp.

   A basic German textbook of military psychology written by the
   scientific director of the High Command's Central Psychological
   Laboratory.

29A. SCHRAMM, Wilbur. et al   The Nature of Psychological Warfare.
Chevy Chase, Md.: John Hopkins Univ., January 1953. 288 pp.

   This book is a general introduction to the principles and
   practice of psychological warfare.

Nature and Theory of P.W.

30. KALIJARVI, Thorsten V. Modern World Politics. New York: Crowell,
1945. 852 pp.

   Essays by 28 contributors on the background and trends of
   international politics. Includes chapters on the press,
   psychological warfare, international espionage and fifth
   columns, and international movements.

31. KISHLER, John P., et al. Rumor, A Review of the Literature. New York: Dunlap, 1952. 121 pp.

>A compendium of information on rumor, giving the origin, uses, diffusion, effects on human behavior, and utilization of rumors in warfare.

32. LERNER, Daniel. ed. Propaganda in War and Crisis. New York: George W. Stewart, 1951. 500 pp.

>The most convenient existing collection of writings on psychological warfare by social scientists, publicists, intelligence and communication specialists, etc. "Several items were prepared especially for this volume; others are declassified war documents here printed for the first time. A substantial number are reprinted from the learned journals and from specialized volumes designed to reach only small professional groups. Several items were taken from current publications." The 27 papers by 24 authors and co-authors are organized into 4 parts: I. "The Twentieth Century Background"; II. "Policy, Intelligence and Propaganda"; III. "The Organization of Purpose and Persons"; and IV. "The Evaluation of Propaganda Effects."

33. MCKENZIE, Vernon. Here Lies Goebbels. London: Joseph, 1940. 319 pp.

>A survey of propaganda from Bismarck to Goebbels, analyzing in detail the propaganda machine of the Third Reich, its technique and effectiveness.

34. SAVA, George, Pseud. War Without Guns; the Psychological Front. London: Faber, 1943. 156 pp.

>All phases of psychological warfare considered. Final chapter is Planned National Psychology.

35. SPEIER, Hans. Social Order and the Risks of War: Papers in Political Sociology. New York: George W. Stewart, 1952. 497 pp.

>Collection of papers written over a twenty-year period by a noted social scientist. Part IV. (pp. 323-455) consists of nine important papers on Political Warfare, including "War Aims in Political Warfare," "'Re-education'--The U.S. Policy," and "Psychological Warfare Reconsidered."

36. STEED, Wickham. The Fifth Arm. London: Constable and Co., 1949 162 pp.

>Essay by a prominent British publicist on the nature and role of propaganda. Chapter headings: I. A War of Faiths; II. The Fifth Army in 1918; III. German Propaganda Before Hitler; IV. German Propaganda under Hitler; V. The Work in Hand; and VI. The Weapon of the Mind.

Books

Tactical and Strategic

37. ALLPORT, Gordon W., and Leo Postman. The Psychology of Rumor. New York: Holt, 1947. 247 pp.

> A comprehensive treatment of rumor by two Harvard psychologists. Includes a discussion of the nature and origins of rumor; the psychological mechanisms involved in its dissemination; its analysis and control; and the role of rumor in propaganda and opinion formation. Based largely on experimental studies of wartime rumors, and the experiences of the OWI and of "rumor clinics."

38. BARRETT, Edward W. Truth is our Weapon. New York: Funk and Wagnalls Co., 1953. 355 pp.

> The importance of psychological warfare; communist propaganda tactics; and the contention that an international campaign of truth — when linked with firm, diplomatic, economic and military politics — can yield vast returns. The faltering progress of international persuasion as conducted by the US Information Service and other propaganda agencies; lessons learned from the experiment; and guides for the future, such as: (1) first rate executives; (2) presidential support and liaison at all levels; and (3) tactical direction on the scene rather than in Washington.

39. BLINOV, I. Ia. O Iazyke Agitatora. (On the Agitator's Language.) Moscow, 1948. 55 pp.

> A handbook for propagandists in the Soviet Armed Forces. It deals with the method of preparing a political lecture, the selection of material, the language to be used, and methods of delivery.

40. CARROLL, Wallace. Persuade or Perish. Boston: Houghton, 1949. 392 pp.

> The strategy and timing of propaganda in relation to military operations. An evaluation of the British and American cooperation in this field during the war.

41. ETTLINGER, Harold. The Axis or the Air. New York: Bobbs-Merrill, 1943. 318 pp.

> Chicago Sun columnist gives an account of German, Japanese, and Italian radio propaganda, 1939-1943, based partly on OWI monitoring records. Contains a chapter each on Soviet, American, and British wartime broadcasts.

Tactical and Strategic (cont'd)　　　　　　　　　　Books

42. FELLERS, Bonner. Thought War Against the Kremlin. Chicago: Henry Regnery Co., 1949. 14 pp.

   The necessity of offensive action in psychological warfare.

43. FRIEDGOOD, Harry B. On the Psycho-Military Nature of Soviet Aggression, with Specific Proposals for a Pro-Democratic Psychological Counteroffensive. Los Angeles: University of California, 1951 110 pp. (Unpublished; dittoed)

   Memorandum by an associate clinical professor of medicine. Part I. "The Pattern and Operational Strategy of Modern Psychological Warfare as Practised by the USSR"; Part II. "Problems Confronting the Democracies in their Search for an ...Approach to the Task of Neutralizing and Destroying the USSR's Psychological Attack"; Part III. "Specific Proposals..." "A Psychiatrically Oriented Expose."

44. FULLER, John F. Maj. Gen. How to Defeat Russia. London: Eyre and Spottiswoode, 1951. 16 pp.

   A British General presents a psychological and military program, based on the psychological offensive. His suggestions include establishment of a central western organ of information and propaganda, and stimulation of resistance movements and the "potential Titoism" which he says exists in all Russian-controlled countries.

45. GOSS, Hilton P. Civilian Morale Under Aerial Bombardment, 1914-1939. Maxwell Air Force Base, Ala.: 1948. 296 pp.

   1. Air University Libraries, Documentary Research Division.

   A detailed, documented account of aerial warfare from the Italo-Turkish war through the Spanish Civil War, designed to assess "reactions of civilian populations." Concludes that no one "could safely say that mass bombardment of civilians would either stiffen or break the will to resist."

46. HOKE, Henry Reed. Black Mail, New York: Raders Book Service, Inc., 1944. 89 pp.

   Before Pearl Harbor, subversive groups in the U.S. used direct mail and the congressional franking privilege for political propaganda purposes. A direct mail advertising expert here describes their activities.

Tactical and Strategic (cont'd)   Books

47. HUSEN, Torsten. Psykologisk Krigforing. (Psychological Warfare).
    Lund, Sweden: Gleerups Forlag, 1942. 127 pp.

    Swedish work on psychological warfare in general, and its role
    in total war in particular, with references to World War I
    activities in the field.

48. LERNER, Daniel. Sykewar. New York: G.W. Stewart, 1949. 461 pp.

    Psychological warfare employed against Germany from D-Day to
    VE-Day. Bibliography included.

49. MACDONALD, Elizabeth P. Undercover Girl. New York: Macmillan,
    1947. 305 pp.

    A personal narrative by a member of the Morale Operations unit
    of the U.S. Office of Strategic Services in China and Southeast
    Asia during World War II. The author had the assignment of
    disseminating rumor and propaganda.

50. PRIESTER, Hans E. Enemy Sponsored News in the Allies Press: A
    Secret Weapon of the Axis. Habana, Cuba: 1943. 110 pp. Unpub.:
    Typescript in LC

    A study of the infiltration of Axis-sponsored news into the Cuban
    press during the early part of World War II. Includes chapters on
    "Enemy-Sponsored News as a Weapon in Total Warfare," "Nazi Army
    Reports," "Political Propaganda of the Nazis," "Italian-
    Sponsored News," and "Japanese Sponsored News." The author suggests
    ways of breaking the Axis new monopoly and utilizing enemy
    reports as an offensive weapon.

51. ROOTHAM, Jasper. Miss Fire. London: Chatto and Windus, 1946.
    224 pp.

    British officer who was parachuted into Yugoslavia in 1943 on a
    mission to Michailovich describes the propaganda techniques
    effectively used by the Nazis to divert Chetnik activities from
    the German army against the partisans.

52. SAVA, George, pseud. War without Guns; the psychological front.

    SEE # 34.

53. SUMMERS, Robert C. ed. America's Weapons of Psychological Warfare.
    New York: Wilson, 1951. 706 pp.

    A collection of articles and speeches concerned with current
    operations of the U.S.I.S. and its effectiveness.

World War I   Books

54. LINEBARGER, Paul M.A. Psychological Warfare. Washington, D.C.: Infantry Journal Press, 1948. 259 pp.

> A standard work by a social scientist long associated with U.S. psychological warfare activities. Surveys the history, definitions and functions of psychological warfare in World Wars I and II: techniques of propaganda analysis and intelligence; and the planning and organization of operations directed at both troops and civilians. Illustrated with many accounts of Allied and Axis activities during World War II.

World War II

55. BONAPARTE, Marie. Myths of War. London: Image, 1947. 161 pp.

> A psychoanalyst discusses rumors and myths of World War II. Examines official and unofficial reports of combat losses, opinions concerning the enemy's strength, and rumors growing from these.

56. BORNSTEIN, Joseph, and Paul R. Milton. Action Against the Enemy's Mind. New York: Bobbs-Merrill, 1942. 294 pp.

> A discussion of psychological warfare, for the layman, focussed on American problems and needs in the early part of World War II. Book I by Bornstein describes the organizations, principles and methods of German psychological warfare. Book II by Milton deals with conditions in American society that tend to cause vulnerability to Axis propaganda. The final chapters deal with American psychological warfare.

57. HOVLAND, Carl, Lumsdaine, Arthur A., and Sheffield, Fred D. Experiments on Mass Communication. Princeton: Princeton University Press, 1949. 345 pp.

> (Vol. III of Studies in Social Psychology in World War II). Important reports on experimental studies of the effectiveness of mass indoctrination of U.S. troops during World War II, done by the Research Branch, Information and Education Division, U.S. War Dept. Suggestive conclusions about the effects of various propaganda materials, media and techniques are presented; the methods by which they were tested are described in detail. Sample topics explored: The relative effectiveness of influencing opinions by presenting "one side", as compared with presenting "both sides", of a controversial issue; the relative effectiveness of an orientation film, "Battle of Britain", in changing specific opinions, as compared with changing general attitudes.

World War II (cont'd)   Books

58. LEAN, Edward Tangye. Voices in the Darkness: The Story of the European Radio War. London: Secker and Warburg, 1943. 243 pp.

    Lively account of selected events, programs, problems, techniques and personalities of World War II radio propaganda, by the editor of the European Service of the BBC. Includes chapters on "The War in German", "The Radio Map", "The War in French", and on British broadcasts to Germany and Italy.

59. MARGOLIN, Leo J. Paper Bullets: A Brief Story of Psychological Warfare in World War II. New York: Froben Press, 1946. 149 pp.

    A journalist's account of French, German, Japanese, and American psychological warfare operations, based on his experience with OWI and the U.S. Army's Psychological Warfare Branch during World War II. Media, themes and effectiveness are discussed. 48 pages of reproductions of psychological warfare materials.

60. MASKELYNE, Jasper. Magic - Top Secret.

    SEE # 25.

61. MCKENZIE, Vernon. Here Lies Goebbels.

    SEE # 33.

62. ROOTHAM, Jasper. Miss Fire.

    SEE # 51.

63. STEED, Wickham. The Fifth Arm.

    SEE # 36.

64. ZACHARIAS, Ellis M. Secret Mission: The Story of an Intelligence Officer. New York: Putnam's, 1946. 433 pp.

    A lively account of the author's experiences in Far East naval intelligence during World War II. Includes a description and assessment of psychological warfare. (Chapter 33, "Decisive Broadcast," is reprinted in # 59). Appendix contains transcripts of 14 propaganda broadcasts Capt. Zacharias made to Japan, May-August 1945.

-12-

DOCUMENTS AND GOV'T PUBLICATIONS

Effects

65. U.S. STRATEGIC BOMBING SURVEY. MORALE DIVISION. *The Effects of Bombing on German Morale.* Washington, D.C.: USGPO, 1946, 1947. Vol. 1-2. 136 and 66 pp.

    Reports on a survey, directed by Rensis Likert, "to determine the direct and indirect effects of bombing upon the attitudes, behavior and health of the civilian population..." Vol. I deals with the reactions of individuals, and is based on interviews with 3,711 German civilians and selected officials, and on official German documents. Points up the fact that lowered morale did not result in active disaffection. Vol. II based primarily on captured German mail, discusses the effect of the bombings on cities or groups of cities. It includes a study of attitudes of foreign workers in Germany, factors affecting DP's adjustment to bombings, the relation of bombings to suicide, and the effects of air attack on the morale of German land armies. Includes data on the validity and reliability of the mail studies.

66. U.S. STRATEGIC BOMBING SURVEY. MORALE DIVISION. *The Effects of Strategic Bombing on Japanese Morale.* Washington, D.C.: USGPO, 1947. 262 pp.

    A report, based on field surveys, of the effects of air raids on the Japanese population and its attitudes toward the war. Devotes special attention to the effects of atom bombs dropped on Hiroshima and Nagasaki.

Mechanical Methods

67. SUPREME HEADQUARTERS, ALLIED EXPEDITIONARY FORCE. Psychological Warfare Division, S.H.A.E.F.: An Account of its Operations in the Western European Campaigns, 1944-1945. Bad Homburg, Germany: SHAEF, Oct. 1945. 243 pp.

    Official history of the administrative structure and activities of this joint Anglo-American organization responsible for the conduct of all psychological warfare in support of military operations in the European Theater. Describes the use of various media. 35-page appendix of official documents, reproduced leaflets, and texts of broadcasts.

Mechanical Methods (cont'd)   Documents & Gov't Publ.

68. U.S. Dept. of the Air Force. Fifth Air Force. DI. Psychological Warfare Program. U.S. Fifth Air Force. Sept. 1952. 39 pp.

    A plan for psychological warfare in Korea. This document contains: a.) Summary of operations; b.) Lists and samples of leaflets; c.) Radio operations; d.) Themes used for broadcasts.

69. U.S. Dept. of the Army. Army Attache. GNA Propaganda Leaflets. Greece: U.S. Dept. of the Army, R-480-49, 1949. 1 pp.

70. Washington Public Opinion Laboratory. Physical Characteristics of Leaflets: A Survey of the literature. Seattle: University of Washington, 1954. 17 pp.

    An investigation of Air Force use of leaflet operations. A survey of the literature relevant to the problem of designing leaflets that will achieve maximum perception in various target populations.

Military Instruction

71. "PSYCHOLOGICAL WARFARE." Fort Knox, Ky.: The Armored School, 1951. V.P.

    History, techniques, organization, and operational procedure of military psychological warfare.

72. Psychological Warfare. Fort Bragg, N.C.: Psychological Warfare School, 1953.

    These are lesson plans provided for the use of instruction to orient personnel in the nature, role, and methods of employing military psychological warfare. (PW 6001) - Historical background of psychological warfare, its nature, objectives and tasks, types of operations, and dissemination media; (PW 6002) - The organization and mission of psychological warfare agencies at national government level, and the organization, mission, capabilities, and equipment of the army PW field operational units; (PW 6003) - PW intelligence, which includes specialized requirements, target and propaganda analysis, and the basic characteristics of propaganda analysis, and the basic characteristics of propaganda, including types, techniques, and symbols; and (PW 6004) - Techniques, characteristics, capabilities, and limitations of radio, leaflet, and loudspeaker operations.

Military Instruction (cont'd) Documents & Gov't Publ.

73. "Radio Broadcasting and Leaflet Group." Fort Bragg, N.C.: Psychological Warfare School, 1953. 7 pp.

    A lesson plan on the organization, mission and equipment of the headquarters and headquarters company, reproduction company, mobile radio broadcast company, and consolidation company. (PW 404 A).

74. "Tactical Psychological Warfare: The Combat Psychological Warfare Detachment." Fort Riley, Kan.: Ground General School, 1948. V.P.

75. U.S. DEPARTMENT OF THE ARMY. Psychological Warfare in Combat Operations. Field Manual FM 33-5. U.S. Dept. of the Army, Aug. 1949.

76. U.S. FIFTH ARMY. Functions of the Fifth Army Combat Propaganda Team. Headquarters, Fifth Army: Psychological Warfare Branch, 1944. 61 pp.

    A declassified training brochure. Reviews the Fifth Army's use of propaganda leaflet shells during combat in Italy. Describes purpose of leaflets, sources of material, writing techniques, themes and appeals, printing, and methods of rolling, converting, and firing shells.

77. U.S. WAR DEPARTMENT. What is Propaganda? Washington, D.C.: USGPO, 1944. 46 pp.

    Illustrated booklet prepared for troop orientation. Contents "approved by the Historical Service Board of the American Historical Association."

78. U.S. War Dept. General Staff. Syllabus of Psychological Warfare. Washington: Propaganda Branch, Intelligence Division, 1946.

Nature and Theory of PW

79. U.S. Dept. of the Army. Human Resources Research Office. Research on Army Psychological Warfare Training. U.S. Dept. of the Army. Dec. 1952. 2 pp.

80. DAVISON, W. Phillips. Some Observations on the Role of Research in Political Warfare. Santa Monica, Cal.: RAND Corp., 1951 (Memorandum P-226.) 30 pp. (Unpubl., dittoed type script.)

    Text of a nontechnical address outlining the meaning of political warfare, the relationship between research and operations, the importance of studying past experience in the field, the application of scientific techniques and concepts, and "Some Criticisms of Political Warfare Research." This is an unpublished, dittoed type script.

Nature & Theory of PW (cont'd)　　　　　　Documents & Gov't Publ.

81. YARNOLD, Kenneth. Fear in Battle. Stamford, Conn.: Dunlap and Associates, March 1951. (Report DA 27-1). V.P.

> This unpublished study is based primarily on a survey of the literature in the field, interpreted in terms of implications for immediate action as well as for future research needs.

Tactical and Strategic

82. MACVEIGH, Maj. Charles S. "Responsibility for Tactical Propaganda- Organic Engineers versus Tactical Propaganda Company." Fort Belvoir, Va.: Engineer School, 1949. 57 pp.

> A thesis on propaganda functions performed at division level in infantry, armored, and airborne divisions. Covers only the possible role of the engineer combat battalion organic to the division. Discusses tactical propaganda, with a description of the organization and utilization of the tactical propaganda company, and the possibility of using the combat engineer battalion to perform all or part of the functions of the same. Recommendation is made that the mission of tactical propaganda be the responsibility of a separate specialized unit, based on: the need for strict control and coordination of propaganda; limited availability of specialist personnel; and possibility of violation of unity of command in the case of an organic propaganda element, span of control, and the principle of homogeneous assignment. Bibliography.

83. U.S. DEPARTMENT OF STATE. Office of Intelligence Research. Strategic Aims of Axis vs. American Broadcasts. Washington, D.C.: Coordinator of information. Psych. Div. Mar. 30, 1942. Report No. 20. 31 pp.

> Comparative study of the strategic aims of broadcasts by the three Axis countries to the U.S., and by the U.S. to them, based on an analysis of scripts over a 6 week sample period. Axis strategy was found to be almost wholly destructive, U.S. propaganda the reverse. The psychological implications of these strategies and the themes used are analyzed. This unpublished material is at the Library of Congress.

84. VATCHER, William H. Jr. Combat Propaganda: Okinawa Campaign. Stanford, Cal.: Stanford University, 1948. (Unpubl. M.A. Thesis) V.P.

85. U.S. ARMY. TWELFTH ARMY GROUP. History: Publicity and Psychological Warfare. European Theatre of Operations: 12th Army Group, 1945. Vol. 1-14. 264 pp.

> Volume 14 is an official history of the activities of the 12th Army Group during World War II.

Tactical and Strategic (cont'd) Documents & Gov't Publ.

86. U.S. Dept. of the Air Force. Air Attache. Psychological Warfare in Norwegian Maneuvers. U.S. Dept. of the Air Force. Sept. 1952. 4 pp.

   A report on the first use of psychological warfare by the Norwegian Armed Forces.

87. U.S. ARMY. EUCOM. I.D. "Psychological Warfare Against U.S.S.R." 30 July 1952. 41 pp.

88. U.S. Eighth Army. Report of the Commanding General, 8th Army, on the Palawan and Zamboanga operation, Victor III and IV. U.S. Eighth Army, 1946. 176 pp.

   Part III, the report of the G-2 Section of the Eighth Army, is devoted to an account of its psychological warfare operations. This is an unpublished study.

89. U.S. First Army. Report of Operations, 23 February to 8 May 1945. Germany: U.S. First Army, 1945. Vol. 1-5. V.P.

   Annex no. 14 of this history is an account of the psychological warfare activities of the First Army.

90. U.S. Third Army. After Action Report, 1 August 1944-9 May 1945. Germany: U.S. Third Army, 1946. Vol. 1-2.

   Volume 2, entitled Staff Section Reports, gives an account of the psychological warfare activities of the Third Army.

World War II

91. GULLAHORN, John T. Selected Propaganda Techniques in German and British Documents in the Early Months of World War II. Los Angeles, Cal.: University of Southern California, 1945. V.P. (Unpub. M.A. thesis)

PERIODICALS

Effects

92. ALLPORT, Floyd H. and Mary M. Simpson. "Broadcasting to an Enemy Country: What Appeals Are Effective, and Why." Journal of Social Psychology. May 1946. Vol. 23, p. 217-24.

   Experimental study of the effectiveness of Axis propaganda themes, based on measured reactions of a university listening group. Students heard recordings of Axis broadcast materials and recorded their acceptance or rejection of various themes. Conclusions regarding American propaganda policy and recommendations for counter-propaganda are presented.

93. CONINE, Ernest. "Psychology Goes to War." Ordnance. May-June 1953. Vol. 37. p. 1055-1059.

   Examples from the Korean War illustrate the effectiveness of psychological warfare as a support weapon. Important information is often gained as a by-product of analyzing enemy propaganda output and interrogating prisoners for psychological warfare purposes.

94. KEHM, H. D. Col. The Methods and Functions of Military Psychological Warfare.

   SEE # 156.

95. KINTNER, William R. "The Effectiveness of Psychological Warfare." Marine Corps Gazette. Jan. 1948. Vol. 32, 48-56 pp.

   U.S. Army officer surveys the role and effectiveness of one aspect of psychological warfare, described as "that aimed at the broad enemy masses, whether military or civilian, through orthodox propaganda media." Describes Allied propaganda against Japan and Germany in World War II, and concludes that "psychological warfare has become an established instrument of war, and rightfully claims due consideration from all those responsible for national security." Reproductions of six World War II propaganda leaflets.

96. MEYER, Georges. La Guerre des Papiers.

   SEE # 119.

Effects (cont'd)   Periodicals

97. "Psychological Effects of Air War." *Air Intelligence Training Bulletin.* Jan. 1954. Vol. 6, p. 34-43.

   The psychological effects of air weapons are new factors in airpower. Differences between psychological warfare and war psychologically waged; types of basic air weapons and their employment for psychological effects; types of psychological effects caused by the air weapons; evaluation of psychological effects; World War II experiences in psychological exploitation of airpower; and methods for waging warfare psychologically during peacetime, among others.

98. "United Nations Command Operations in Korea." *Dept. of State Bulletin.* Mar. 19, 1951. Vol. 24, p. 470-74.

   Comments on the effectiveness of over 205 leaflets which were disseminated. Information on the seven United Nations radio stations which serve to counteract Communist broadcasts from the USSR and China.

Korean War

99. AVEDON, Herbert. Capt. "War for Men's Minds."

   SEE # 153.

100. DAVISON, W. Philips. "Air Force Psychological Warfare in Korea." *Air University Quarterly Review.* 1951. Vol. 4. p. 40-48.

   The chief reasons why the Air Force did not play a more active role in conventional psychological warfare in Korea were non-existance of organizational conditions and extensive shortages in materials, equipment, and personnel. However, appearance of friendly aircraft encouraged South Korean leaders as well as the South Korean population at critical moments. Air activity exerted powerful psychological effects on enemy troops, and air support contributed greatly to the morale of the UN troops. Air activity in Korea has indicated a number of principles regarding psychological effects which will probably hold true in other situations. A few of these principles are discussed.

101. GALLANT, Roy A. "Why Red Troops Surrender in Korea." *The Reporter.* 5 Aug. 1952. Vol. 7, p. 19-21.

   Article describes the success of psychological warfare on Communist soldiers who surrender because of propaganda fatigue, lack of food, and lack of medical care.

102. KARLSTAD, Charles H. The Psywar Center Story.

   SEE # 135.

Korean War (cont'd)   Periodicals

103. "Psychological Warfare in Korea, an Interim Report."

   SEE # 128.

104. STORY, Dale. Psywar in Korea.

   SEE # 129.

Mechanical Methods

105. BRYDIA, Charles. "Psychological Warfare." Quartermaster Review.
     Jan.-Feb. '54. Vol. 33, p. 26-27.

   Activities of the Research and Development Division, Office of the
   Quartermaster General, in developing, printing, and composing
   machines for reproduction of foreign languages on paper. Also
   describes the process of preparation and delivery of leaflets
   across the enemy lines, as part of the Psychological Warfare
   Program, in order to break down the enemy's morale and will to
   resist and to induce him to surrender.

106. DE MENT, Jack. "Substitute Atomic Warfare." Military Engineer.
     Jan.-Feb. 1952. Vol. 44, p. 10-13.

107. GASK, Roland C. "Japs Do Surrender." Newsweek. Oct. 30, 1944.
     Vol. 24, p. 31-33.

   A Newsweek war correspondent describes American psychological
   warfare activities in the China-Burma-India theater during World
   War II. Mentions some of the appeals and methods used in the
   struggle to break through the Japanese mentality, including
   leaflets and surrender passes.

108. GASKEY, Edward A. Maj. "Baloney Barrage." Infantry Journal. Dec.
     1949. Vol. 62.

   Account of a U.S. tactical propaganda operation on the Western
   front in 1944. Leaflet shells and loudspeakers were used to
   urge the surrender of a German garrison.

109. GRENIER, Raymond. "Presse Aeroportee de Guerre: Vie et Mort du
     Courrier des Nations Unies." Etudes de Presse. April-March 1946.
     Vol. 1, p. 316-319.

   French journalist gives humorous account of the circumstances
   under which a U.S.-British-French team, set up jointly by the
   Psychological Warfare Branch and the Free French Commissariat
   a l'Information, put out a leaflet-type "newspaper" for airborne
   distribution in Southern France in 1944. Scene of operations
   Algiers.

Mechanical Methods (cont'd)   Periodicals

110. HADLEY, A. "The Propaganda Tank'." *Armor*. Jan-Feb. 1951. Vol. 60, p. 32-33.

   Brief account of the use of tank-mounted loudspeakers in combat propaganda, by a former psychological warfare officer who pioneered their development for tactical use.

111. HANSER, Richard. "Ist ein Scherz, Sohn!" *Infantry Journal*. Sept. 1946. Vol. 59, p. 62-63.

   Brief account of the U.S. Army's use of jokes as a propaganda device in World War II, by a U.S. serviceman who told anti-Nazi jokes over Radio Luxembourg.

112. HARALDSEN, S. "Psychological Warfare." *Military Review*. Jan. 1950. Vol. 29, p. 78-83.

   Describes the use of psychological warfare by the Germans against the French at the Maginot Line. Illustrations of German and Japanese leaflets.

113. HERZ, Martin F. "Some Psychological Lessons from Leaflet Propaganda." *Public Opinion Quarterly*. Fall 1949. Vol. 13, p. 471-486.

   Former chief leaflet writer for the Psychological Warfare Division of SHAEF offers a set of principles to guide the combat propagandist. He discusses the judging of effectiveness, handling of defeats, dangers of black propaganda, appeals to the unconscious, use of threats, and propaganda to civilians.

114. HERZ, Martin F. "The Combat Leaflet: Weapon of Persuasion." *Army Information Digest*. June 1950. Vol. 5, p. 37-43.

   This article sets forth the principles of leaflet writing, with specific examples drawn from both Axis and Allied propaganda leaflet operations. Texts of several leaflets are reproduced.

115. ISRAELS, Joseph. "The Wehrmacht's Yankee Girlfriend." *Colliers* 3 Mar. 1945. Vol. 115, 68 pp.

   Description of the "Music with Margaret" program which the OWI broadcast to German soldiers during World War II.

116. JOSEPHY, Alvin M., Jr. "Some Japs Surrender." *Infantry Journal*. Aug. 1945. Vol. 58, p. 40-45.

   Marine combat correspondent describes the use of leaflets, sound trucks and a "sound-ship" to persuade Japanese troops to surrender during the battle of Guam. He also reports a conversation on the subject with Japanese prisoners of war.

Mechanical Methods (cont'd)　　　　　　　　　　Periodicals

117. JURIST, Stewart S. "Leaflets Over Europe: Allied Propaganda Used Some Advertising Principles." *Printers Ink*. Oct. 26, 1945. Vol. 213, p. 23-24.

   Summary of the propaganda themes used in leaflets of the Psychological Warfare Branch of SHAEF. Five leaflets are reproduced.

118. KEHM, H. D., Col. "The Methods and Functions of Military Psychological Warfare." *Military Review*. Jan. 1947. Vol. 26, p. 3-15.

   Discusses Allied World War II radio operations, leaflet writing, pictures, books and posters.

119. MEYER, Georges. "La Guerre des Papiers." *L'Armee Francaise*. March 1948. Vol. 24, p. 29-36.

   Former director of the Press and Propaganda Section of the French Ministry of War discusses the use of leaflets and other media in psychological warfare between France and Germany during World Wars I and II. Includes sections on the history and effectiveness of "paper warfare" and the aims of French propaganda.

120. MORGAN, B. "Operation Annie; Army radio station that fooled the Nazis by telling them the truth." *The Saturday Evening Post*. March 9, 1946, p. 18-19 plus.

   An account of the black radio propaganda campaign of the Allies beamed to Munich during World War II.

121. NICHOLS, Maynard. "All the News in Japanese." *New York Times Magazine*. Jan. 7, 1945, p. 20.

   Describes the contents of a newspaper-style U.S. propaganda leaflet dropped over Formosa in October 1944.

122. O'NEILL, Col. "Paper Warfare in Tunisia." *Army Quarterly*. (London) April 1944. Vol. 48, p. 81-89.

   Discussion of the use of leaflets in front-line propaganda by a British officer engaged in military propaganda in North Africa during World War II. He developed the "propaganda shell" for the Allied Troops. Reviews some problems involved in propaganda organization, the relation of the propagandist to his army, production in the field, and various methods of distribution, with emphasis on the advantages of the shell.

Mechanical Methods (cont'd)   Periodicals

123. PAINTON, Frederick C. "Fighting with Confetti." Reader's Digest. Dec. 1943. Vol. 43, p. 99-101.

   Story of the psychological warfare branch in the Sicilian campaign credited with saving American lives.

124. "Paper Bombs in Korea." New York Times Magazine. Feb. 25, 1951, p. 46-47.

   Reproductions of six leaflets, prepared by the U.S. Army's Psychological Warfare Division, illustrating major U.S. propaganda themes.

125. PENA, Ambrosia P., Capt. Psychological Warfare on Bataan.

   SEE # 176.

126. PRINGLE, Henry F. "The 'Baloney Barrage' Pays Off." Saturday Evening Post. March 31, 1945. Vol. 217, p. 18-19 plus.

   A journalist reviews the media and techniques used by U.S. psychological warfare units in various campaigns during World War II.

127. "Psychological Warfare."

   SEE # 161.

128. "Psychological Warfare in Korea, an Interim Report." Public Opinion Quarterly. 1951. Vol. 15, p. 65-75.

   A preliminary account of United Nations psychological warfare activities during the first phase of the Korean war. Since it was written prior to the large scale entry of Chinese forces into the fighting, it deals only with leaflet, radio, and other forms of propaganda directed to Korean soldiers and civilians during the six month period from June to December, 1950.

129. STORY, Dale. "Psywar in Korea." Combat Forces Journal. July 1952. Vol. 2, p. 25-27.

   Psychological warfare methods, techniques, and equipment by the US Eighth Army to induce Communist soldiers to surrender to our forces, and examples of tactical advantages gained through the application of these methods; contents of our propaganda leaflets; the failure of Chinese communist psychological warfare methods in contrast to our success; and the impetus given to psychological warfare training in the US Army by experience gained in Korea.

Mechanical Methods (cont'd)   Periodicals

130. WEAVER, John O., Lt. Col.   "Stock Number 56-C-13065-H." *Military Review*. Jan.-Feb. 1953. Vol. 32, p. 45-46 plus.

> "56-C-13065-H" was a cigarette distributed to North Korean and Chinese army prisoners in UN camps. The design and messages on the container were prepared after a study which aimed to penetrate the regimented minds of the Communists.

Military Instruction

131. "Army Psychological Warfare." *Officer's Call*. 1950. Vol. 2, p. 1-11.

> This article is intended to give military personnel a general picture of psychological warfare agencies and individuals, the tools with which they work, and what they can and cannot do to help our ground troops accomplish their missions.

132. CASSEL, Maj. Russell N.   "Psychological Warfare." *Military Review*. Nov. 1953. p. 58-62.

> Describes plans that should be put into operation for educating military personnel in the theories of psychological warfare. Effective psychological warfare is totally dependent upon satisfactory communications with the enemy population, both civilian and military. Countermeasures to be employed are: 1) propaganda analysis, and 2) propaganda intelligence.

133. CONINE, Ernest. "New Horizons in Psychological Warfare." *Army Information Digest*. Dec. 1952. Vol. 7, p. 21-27.

> The development of military psychological warfare, and the importance attached to it by the USSR. Rapid expansion of the US Army's Psychological Warfare Division after the outbreak of the Korean conflict, and the role it has taken in the fighting. Describes training program at the Psychological Warfare Center, Fort Bragg, N.C., qualifications for officers and enlisted men for assignment to this duty, the basic units used in US Army psychological operations, and their functions.

Military Instruction (cont'd)   Periodicals

134. HALL, Donald F. "Organization for Combat Propaganda." *Army Information Digest*. May 1951. Vol. 6, p. 11-16.

   Taking advantage of the lessons learned in combat during World War II, psychological warfare units have been reorganized, with strategic and tactical functions allocated to separate units. Strategic Group units include Radio Broadcasting and Leaflet Group, consisting of Group Headquarters and Headquarters Company, the Reproduction Company, and the Mobile Radio Broadcasting Company. The three companies are now operating under Tables of Distribution, but steps are under way to convert them to T/O & E status. The Loudspeaker and Leaflet Company, the new tactical organization, consists of the Publications Platoon, the Propaganda Platoon, and the Loudspeaker Platoon. Data are presented on the mission, strength, equipment, and operations of each of the units enumerated. Combat propaganda operations in the future and the Army's current psychological warfare program are expected to derive a vastly increased efficiency from recent research and development in the field of printing and electronics. A comprehensive program for training new specialists is under way, and operational units are functioning in training camps and in combat.

135. KARLSTAD, Charles H. "The Psywar Center Story." *Army-Navy-Air Force Journal*. Nov. 1952. Vol. 90, p. 249.

   The Commanding Officer of the Psychological Warfare Center, Fort Bragg, N.C., briefly reviews the psychological warfare aspects of the Korean conflict, and the rapid mobilization of experts immediately after the outbreak of hostilities. More than fifteen million leaflets each week are sent into Communist cities, villages, and military installations; twelve Korean radio transmitters are being operated; and there are nineteen more shortwave broadcasting outlets in Japan. Describes the program of training officers for psychological warfare which was begun at the Army General School at Fort Riley, Kans., and later moved to Fort Bragg, and the main phases of activity at the Center.

136. KEHM, Col. H. D. "Organization for Military Psychological Warfare in ETO." *Military Review*. Feb. 1947. Vol. 26, p. 10-15.

   The organization of the Psychological Warfare Division of SHAEF in the European Theatre of Operations.

137. MCCLURE, Brig. Gen. Robert A. "Psychological Strategy as a Preventative of a Large War." *U.S. News and World Report*. 2 Jan. 1953. Vol. 2, p. 60-69.

   Purpose and objectives, techniques and means of psychological warfare. Its capabilities as an instrument of cold war and a weapon in the event of a war with the USSR.

Military Instruction   Periodicals

138. MCCLURE, Brig. Gen. Robert A. "Psychological Warfare." Army-Navy-Air Force Journal. Jan. 13, 1951. Vol. 88, p. 517, 537.

> An outline of the organization and functions of the Office of the Chief of Psychological Warfare in the Department of the Army, by its Chief, a career soldier with many years' experience in psychological warfare. Describes operational plans at both the staff and field levels, including the responsibilities of each of the four divisions of his Office. Brief mention of psychological warfare operations in Korea.

139. "Military Psychology." Psychological Bulletin. (Washington) June 1941. Vol. 38.

> A collection of essays on all phases of military psychology.

140. "Psychological Warfare." Army-Navy-Air Force Journal. Oct. 1950. Vol. 88, p. 168.

> Outlines functions of new Psychological Warfare Division Special Staff.

141. WILMOT, Fred W. "The Infantry and Psychological Warfare." Infantry School Quarterly. Oct. 1952. Vol. 41, p. 100-104.

> Role played by combat PsyWar in support of the infantry, and steps to be taken by infantry commanders to receive such support.

142. "Your Defense Against Enemy Propaganda." Armed Forces Talk. USGPO. 24 Oct. 1952. 15 pp.

> Information to acquaint personnel with enemy propaganda and with some methods of defense against it.

Nature and Theory of P.W.

143. BELLAK, Leopold. "The Nature of Slogans." Journal of Abnormal and Social Psychology. Oct. 1942. Vol. 37, p. 497-510.

> Harvard social psychologist reviews studies in the field and discusses current war slogans.

Nature and Theory of P.W. (cont'd)　　　　　　　Periodicals

144. CESAR, E. P. "Aspecto psiccologico e profilaxia da guerra de nervos." (Psychological aspect and prophylaxis in a war of nerves.) *Imprensa Medica*. (Rio de Janeiro.) 1945. Vol. 21, p. 69-71.

   Traces the history of psychological warfare from the use of tatoos, black paint and sound instruments by savages to present officially sponsored and mechanized methods. Considers the basic objectives of a war of nerves to be the creation of fear, disunity and demoralization in the enemy, and the creation of one's own side of a uniting ideology causing the individual to identify himself with the collective super ego.

145. GERADOT, P. "La Guerre Moderne st. le Principle d'Economie des Forces." *Revue de Defense Nationale*. Feb. 1949. Vol. 5, p. 147-164.

   Discusses the use of psychological warfare as a means of conserving military resources.

146. HARGREAVES, Maj. Reginald. "The Fourth Arm." *The Army Quarterly*. Apr. 1953. Vol. 66, p. 33-44.

   Examples of employment of propaganda in ancient times, during and after the French Revolution, during the American Revolution and Civil War, in World War I, and in the period between the two World Wars. The safest and most effective use of propaganda is through presentation of facts and truth. Lies boomerang on those who use them.

147. MAHONEY, Tom. "Words That Win Battles." *Popular Science*. June 1945. Vol. 146, p. 206-207.

   Illustrated popular article on the advantage of psychological warfare, emphasizing the use of surrender leaflets.

148. "Psychological Warfare." *Officer's Call*. N.D. Vol. 4, p. 2-9.

   The ideological aspects of psychological warfare as inherent in the struggle of the free world against Communism. Totalitarian methods and objectives vs. U.S. methods and objectives; truth and falsehood as tools of psychological warfare; objectives of psychological strategy; and functions of the U.S. Psychological Strategy Board established in 1951. Military personnel of any armed force are the targets of the enemy's psychological warfare; and U.S. officers must study the subject in order to be able to deal with it intelligently, as well as to protect enlisted men and counteract any effects which enemy propaganda may have upon them.

Nature and Theory of P.W. (cont'd)　　　　　　Periodicals

149. SAFFORD, Wallace F. "An Appraisal of Psychological Warfare as an Instrument of National Policy." *U.S. Air Force, DI.* 1953. 59 pp.

   The potentialities of psychological warfare. Background of historical development, and its use in World War II; the basic characteristics of psychological warfare, and the intelligence functions it requires. Conclusions and bibliography.

150. SPEIER, Hans. "Psychological Warfare Reconsidered." RAND Corp. Feb. 1951. 30 pp.

   A comprehensive study of psychological warfare and propaganda.

151. WHITE, Ralph K. "Hitler, Roosevelt, and the Nature of War Propaganda." *Journal of Abnormal and Social Psychology.* April 1949. Vol. 44, p. 157-174.

   "In order to throw light on the actual nature of 'propaganda for war,' as distinguished from propaganda in general, the value-analysis technique was applied to a sample, (1935-1939), of Hitler's pre-war speeches and to a comparable sample of speeches by Roosevelt." Conclusions are tentatively applied to an evaluation of Soviet propaganda.

Tactical and Strategic

152. ARSENIAN, Seth. "Wartime Propaganda in the Middle East." *Middle East Journal.* Oct. 1948. Vol. 2, p. 417-430.

   Account of Axis and Allied efforts since 1935.

153. AVEDON, Herbert, Capt. "War for Men's Minds." *Military Review.* March 1954. Vol. 33, p. 53-60.

   The importance of psychological warfare in the present world situation, and some of the factors influencing propaganda. Truth is the most effective weapon available to the United Nations in their fight against Communism. Some aspects of tactical psychological warfare during the Korean conflict.

154. "Communist Propaganda." *Armed Forces Talk.* 7 Mar. 1952. 15 pp.

   The first of two articles on this subject, aims, methods, degree of effectiveness, and what the U.S. is doing officially or through unofficial channels to counteract it. The first part covers the organization and dissemination of propaganda in the Soviet Union, and organization and policies of communist propaganda outside the USSR.

Tactical and Strategic (cont'd)   Periodicals

155. DOOB, Leonard W. "The Strategies of Psychological Warfare." *Public Opinion Quarterly*. (Winter 1949-50) Vol. 13, p. 635-644.

> Yale psychologist, a one-time OWI official, seeks to demonstrate that the strategies of PW are reducible to a finite number of types, by offering a method of considering systematically the possible responses of the target audience.

156. KEHM, H. D., Col. "The Methods and Functions of Military Psychological Warfare." *Military Review*. Jan.-March 1947. Vol. 26, V. P.

> Series of articles by a one-time Military Deputy to the Chief of SHAEF's Psychological Warfare Division. The first discusses concepts of psychological warfare, interrelations between its political and military aspects, black propaganda, media, methods, intelligence requirements, and the control of information in enemy and liberated countries. The second outlines the organization and functions of psychological warfare agencies in the European Theater during World War II and discusses such problems as personnel, logistics and communications. The third "examines various criteria for measuring the effect of psychological warfare operations (interrogations, observer reports, enemy counter-measures, etc.) and deduces some general lessons from past experience.

157. KOTEN, B. L. "The Soviet Artist Joins the War Effort." *American Review of the Soviet Union*. (New York) Feb. 1942. p. 13-28.

> The psychological warfare campaigns of TASS during the days of the German invasion.

158. KRUGMAN, Morris and S. Silverman. "Psychological Weapons of War." *Mental Hygiene*. July 1942. Vol. 26, p. 461-468.

> Offensive and defensive psychological warfare.

159. MENEFEE, Selden C. "Propaganda Wins Battles." *The Nation*. Feb. 12, 1944. Vol. 158, p. 184-186.

> Journalistic description of U.S. psychological warfare methods used in North Africa, Sicily, and Southern Italy during World War II. Gives examples of strategic, tactical, and "mopping-up", or occupation, propaganda.

160. PETERS, Maj. Bernard. "USAF and Psychological Warfare." *Air University Quarterly Review*. 1949. p. 3-16.

> Relationship between air warfare and psychological warfare. An analysis of the ways in which the USAF can best support combat psychological warfare operations.

Tactical and Strategic (cont'd)   Periodicals

161. "Psychological Warfare." Infantry School Quarterly. July 1947. Vol. 31, p. 77-94.

> Discussion of objectives and tactics of propaganda in support of military operations. Texts of several Allied propaganda leaflets are reproduced.

162. SLEEPER, Raymond S. "Air Power, the Cold War, and Peace." Air University Quarterly Review. 1951-52. Vol. 5, p. 2-18.

> Air power as a psychological weapon. Political-psychological victories similar to the successful Berlin Airlift can be obtained by the Strategic Air Force. Reviews the historical use of air power, its effect upon populations, and its success in producing desired reactions by an enemy. For example, airlifting wheat to India would have identified air power as peace power that is friendly to our allies. Concludes that our great strategic air power today must be used to wage peace through air persuasion while it is still superior to Soviet strategic air power.

163. WIMOT, Fred W. The Infantry and Psychological Warfare.

> SEE # 141.

World War I

164. MEYER, Georges. La Guerre des Papiers.

> SEE # 119.

World War II

165. BECKER, Howard. "The Nature and Consequences of Black Propaganda." American Sociological Review. April 1949. Vol. 14, p. 221-235.

> Sociologist who worked with O.S.S. during World War II gives descriptive summary of main types of black propaganda used, with special attention to radio. He expresses views on the probable degree of usefulness of such propaganda.

166. GASK, Roland C. Japs Do Surrender.

> SEE # 107.

World War II (cont'd)　　　　　　　　　　　Periodicals

167. GULLAHORN, John T. "Propaganda Techniques in German Documents During World War I." *Sociology and Social Research*. March-Apr. 1946. Vol. 30, p. 290-302.

   Short, non-technical descriptions of German propaganda devices, based on an examination of German documents. These deal with the use of "color words"; appeal to stereotypes; appeal to emotions; "glittering generalities"; "authentication"; "name-calling"; atrocity stories; contrast; "divide and conquer"; identification; the "plain folks technique"; and "transfer."

168. HERZ, Martin F. "Psychological Warfare Against Surrounded Troop Units." *Military Review*. Aug. 1950. Vol. 30, p. 3-9.

   Psychological warfare expert examines the effectiveness of various techniques used against surrounded enemy troops during World War II. Concludes that ultimata and attacks on enemy commanders are ineffectual, that premature surrender appeals may stiffen the enemy's will to resist, and that "leaflets assuring the troops good treatment if captured are likely to have some effect."

169. KEHM, H.D., Col. The Methods and Functions of Military Psychological Warfare.

   SEE # 118.

170. KINTNER, William R. The Effectiveness of Psychological Warfare.

   SEE # 95.

171. LINEBARGER, Paul M. A. "Psychological Warfare in World War Two." *Infantry Journal*. May 1947. Vol. 60, p. 30-39.

   A review of German propaganda before World War II, the British-German radio war, and American propaganda operations. Japanese, Soviet and Chinese propaganda activities are mentioned. Concludes with a discussion of "Psychological Warfare in the Future."

172. "Meet Psychological Warfare." *Armed Forces Talk, No. 303*. USGPO. 1949. 11 pp.

   An outline of functions of a psychological warfare division. The uses of psychological warfare during World War II are briefly summarized.

173. MEYER, Georges. La Guerre Papiers.

   SEE # 119.

World War II (cont'd)   Periodicals

174. MILLER, Moscrip. "Talking Them Out of It." Colliers. Aug. 19, 1944. Vol. 114, p. 23, 72-73.

   Brief account of the work of OWI's Psychological Warfare Branch during World War II, especially in Italy. Cites examples of the successful use of surrender leaflets and safe conduct passes.

175. O'NEILL, Col. Paper Warfare in Tunisia.

   SEE # 122.

176. PENA, Ambrosia P., Capt. "Psychological Warfare on Bataan." Philippine Armed Forces Journal. Apr. 1953. p. 8-9.

   Japanese psychological warfare methods in the Philippines during the initial stages of World War II. Contents of radio broadcasts and printed matter addressed to U.S. and Philipino troops; misrepresentation of historical facts in order to arouse hatred against the Americans; and the reasons why the Japanese propaganda effort was a complete failure.

177. PRINGLE, Henry F. The 'Baloney Barrage' Pays Off.

   SEE # 126.

178. "Psychological Warfare." Military Review. Jan. 1950. Vol. 29, p. 78-83.

   This article was translated and digested by the Military Review from an article by Commander S. Haraldsen in Militaer Orientering (Norway), No. 10, 1949. Weighs the lessons to be drawn from psychological warfare experiences during World War II by countries with limited resources like Norway. Includes facsimiles of a German and a Japanese propaganda leaflet used at Anzio and Okinawa respectively.

179. "Psychological Warfare and the Soldier." Military Review. Oct. 1949. Vol. 29, p. 73-78.

   Digested by the Military Review from an article in the Australian Army Journal, Aug.-Sept. 1948. A comparison of psychological warfare campaigns and methods of the Allies and Axis powers in World War II.

AUTHOR-TITLE INDEX

(Numbers refer to items, not pages)

ALLPORT, Gordon W. Psychology of Rumor	37
"ARMY PSYCHOLOGICAL WARFARE." Officer's Call	131
ARSENIAN, Seth. "Wartime Propaganda in the Middle East." Middle East Journal.	152
AVEDON, Herbert. Capt. "War for Men's Minds." Military Review.	153
BARRETT, Edward W. Truth is our Weapon.	38
BECKER, Howard. "The Nature and Consequences of Black Propaganda." American Sociological Review.	165
BELLAK, Leopold. "The Nature of Slogans." Journal of Abnormal and Social Psychology.	143
BLINOV, I. Ia. O Iazyke Agitatora. (On the Agitator's Language.)	39
BONAPARTE, Marie. Myths of War	55
BORNSTEIN, Joseph. Action Against the Enemy's Mind.	56
BRYDIA, Charles. Psychological Warfare. QM Rev.	105
CARROLL, Wallace. Persuade or Perish.	40
CASSEL, Major. Russel N. "Psychological Warfare." Military Review.	132
CESAR, E. P. "Aspecto pisiccologico e profilaxia da guerra de nervos." (Psychological aspect and prophylaxis in a war of nerves. Imprensa Medica. (Rio de Janeiro.)	144
CHUBAK, Benjamin. Bibliography of Morale.	1
COFFEY, Lt. Col. J. I. "Psychological Warfare Bibliography." Term Papers and Book Reports	2

"COMMUNIST PROPAGANDA." Armed Forces Talk.	154
CONINE, Ernest. "Psychology Goes to War." Ordance.	93
CONINE, Ernest. "New Horizations in Psychological Warfare. Army Information Digest.	133
DAVISON, W. Phillips. Some Observations on the Role of Research in Political Warfare.	80
DAVISON, W. Philips. "Air Force Psychological Warfare in Korea." Air University Quarterly Review.	100
DE MENT, Jack. "Substitute Atomic Warfare." Military Engineer.	106
DOOB, Leonard W. "The Strategies of Psychological Warfare." Public Opinion Quarterly.	155
ETTLINGER, Harold. The Axis on the Air.	41
FARAGO, Ladislas, ed. German Psychological Warare; Survey and Bibliography	3
FELLERS, Bonner. Thought War Against the Kremlin.	42
FRIEDGOOD, Harry B. On the Psycho-Military Nature of Soviet Aggression	43
FULLER, John F. Maj. Gen. How to Defeat Russia.	44
GALLANT, Roy A. "Why Red Troops surrender in Korea." The Reporter.	101
GASIOROWSKI, Janusz. Bibliographie De Psychologie Militaire.	4
GASK, Roland C. "Japs Do Surrender." Newsweek.	107
GASKEY, Edward A. Maj. "Baloney Barrage." Infantry Journal.	108
GERADOT, P. "La Guerre Moderne et le Principe d'Economie des Forces." Revue de Defense Nationale.	145
GILBERT, Harry T. "Bibliography on Psychological Warfare."	5
GOSS, Hilton P. Civilian Morale Under Aerial Bombardment, 1914-1939.	45
GRENIER, Raymond. "Presse Aeroportee de Guerre: Vie et Mort du Courrier des Nations Unies." Etudes de Presse.	109
GULLAHORN, John T. Selected Propaganda Techniques in German and British Documents in the Early Months of World War II.	91
GULLAHORN, John T. Propaganda Techniques in German Documents during World War II.	167

HADLEY, A.	"The Propaganda Tank." Armor.	110
HALL, Donald F.	"Organization for Combat Propaganda." Army Information Digest.	134
HANSER, Richard.	"Ist ein Scherz, Sohn!" Infantry Journal.	111
HARGREAVES, Maj. Reginald.	"The Fourth Arm." The Army Quarterly.	146
HARDLSEN, S.	"Psychological Warfare." Military Review.	112
HARTER, D. Lincoln.	Propaganda Handbook.	17
HERZ, Martin F.	"Some Psychological Lessons from Leaflet Propaganda." Public Opinion Quarterly.	113
HERZ, Martin F.	"The Combat Leaflet; Weapon of Persuasion." Army Information Digest.	114
HERZ, Martin F.	"Psychological Warfare Against Surrounded Troop Units." Military Review.	168
HOKE, Henry Reed.	Black Mail.	46
HOVLAND, Carl.	Experiments on Mass Communication.	57
HUMMEL, William.	The Analysis of Propaganda.	19
HUNTRESS, Keith.	The Analysis of Propaganda.	19
HUSEN, Torsten.	Militar Psykologi. (Military Psychology.)	26
HUSEN, Torsten.	Psychologisk Krigforing. (Psychological Warfare.)	47
ISRAELS, Joseph.	"The Wehrmacht's Yankee Girlfriend." Colliers.	115
JANIS, Irving.	Air War and Emotional Stress.	14
JOSEPHY, Alvin M., Jr.	"Some Japs Surrender." Infantry Journal.	116
JURIST, Stewart S.	"Leaflets Over Europe: Allied Propaganda Used Some Advertising Principles." Printers Ink.	117
KALIJARVI, Thorsten V.	Modern World Politics	30
KAMINS, B. F.	Basic Propaganda	20
KARLSTAD, Charles H.	"The Psywar Center Story." Army-Navy-Air Force Journal.	135

KEHM, H.D. Col.	"The Methods and Functions of Military Psychological Warfare." Military Review.	118
KEHM, Col. H.D.	"Organization for Military Psychological Warfare in ETO." Military Review.	136
KEHM, H.D. Col.	The Methods and Functions of Military Psychological Warfare.	156
KINTNER, William R.	"The Effectiveness of Psychological Warfare." Marine Corps Gazette.	95
KISHLER, John P.	Rumor, a Review of the Literature.	31
KOTEN, B. L.	"The Soviet Artist joins the War Effort." American Review of the Soviet Union. (New York)	157
SMITH, Bruce Lannes; Lasswell, Harold D.; and Casey, Ralph D.	Propaganda, Communication, and Public Opinion: A Comprehensive Reference Guide.	9
LASSWELL, Harold D.	Propaganda Technique in the World War.	27
LEAN, Edward Tangye.	Voices in the Darkness: The Story of the European Radio War.	58
LERNER, Daniel.	Sykerwar.	6
LERNER, Daniel. ed.	Propaganda in War and Crisis.	32
LERNER, Daniel.	Sykewar.	48
LINEBARGER, Paul M.A.	Psychological Warfare.	54
LINEBARGER, Paul M. A.	"Psychological Warfare in World War Two." Infantry Journal.	171
LUMSDAINE, Arthur A.	Experiments of Mass Communication.	57
McCLURE, Brig. Gen. Robert A.	"Psychological Strategy as a Preventative of a Large War." U.S. News and World Report.	137
MCCLURE, Brig. Gen. Robert A.	"Psychological Warfare. Army-Navy-Air Force Journal.	138
MCKENZIE, Vernon.	Here Lies Goebbels.	33
MACDONALD, Elizabeth P.	Undercover Girl.	49
MACVEIGH, Maj. Charles S.	"Responsibility for Tactical Propaganda - Organic Engineers versus Tactical Propaganda Company."	82

MAHONEY, Tom. "Words That Win Battles." Popular Science.	147
MARGOLIN, Leo J. Paper Bullets: A Brief Story of Psychological Warfare in World War II.	59
MASKELYNE, Jasper. Magic - Top Secret.	25
"Meet Psychological Warfare." Armed Forced Talk. No. 303, (Washington)	172
MENEFEE, Selden C. "Propaganda Wins Battles." The Nation.	159
MEYER, Georges. "La Guerre des Papiers." L'Armee Francaise.	119
"Military Psychology." Psychological Bulletin. (Washington)	139
MILLER, Moscrip. "Talking Them Out of It." Colliers.	174
BORNSTEIN, Joseph, and Paul R. Milton. Action Against the Enemy's Mind.	18
MILTON, Paul R. Action Against the Enemy's Mind.	56
MORGAN, B. "Operation Annie; Army radio station that fooled the Nazis by telling them the truth." The Saturday Evening Post.	120
NATIONAL RESEARCH COUNCIL. Psychology for the Armed Services	28
NICHOLS, Maynard. "All the News in Japanese." New York Times Magazine.	121
O'NEILL, Col. "Paper Warfare in Tunisia." Army Quarterly.	122
PAINTON, Frederick C. "Fighting with Confetti." Reader's Digest.	123
"PAPER BOMBS IN KOREA." New York Times Magazine.	124
PENA, Ambrosia P. Capt. "Psychological Warfare on Bataan." Philippine Armed Forces Journal.	176
PETERS, Maj. Bernard. "USAF and Psychological Warfare." Air University Quarterly Review.	160
POSTMAN, Leo Psychology of Rumor.	37
PRIESTER, Hans E. Enemy Sponsored News in the Allies Press: A Secret Weapon of the Axis.	50
PRINGLE, Henry F. "The 'Baloney Barrage' Pays Off." Saturday Evening Post.	126
"PSYCHOLOGICAL EFFECTS OF AIR WAR." Air Intelligence Training Bulletin.	97
"PSYCHOLOGICAL WARFARE."	71

"PSYCHOLOGICAL WARFARE."	72
"PSYCHOLOGICAL WARFARE." Army-Navy-Air Force Journal.	140
"PSYCHOLOGICAL WARFARE." Infantry School Quarterly.	161
"PSYCHOLOGICAL WARFARE." Military Review	178
"PSYCHOLOGICAL WARFARE." Officers' Call.	148
"PSYCHOLOGICAL WARFARE AND THE SOLDIER." Military Review.	179
"Psychological Warfare Aginst USSR."	87
"PSYCHOLOGICAL WARFARE IN KOREA, AN INTERIM REPORT." Public Opinion Quarterly.	128
"Psychological Warfare in Support of Military Operations."	7
"RADIO BROADCASTING AND LEAFLET GROUP."	73
ROOTHAM, Jasper. Miss Fire.	51
SAFFORD, Wallace F. "An Appraisal of Psychological Warfare as an Instrument of National Policy." U. S. Air Force, DI.	149
SAVA, George, Pseud. War without Guns; the psychological front.	34
SCHRAMM, Wilbur. The Nature of Psychological Warfare.	29a
SHEFFIELD, Fred D. Experiments on Mass Communication.	57
KRUGMAN, Morris and S. Silverman. "Psychological Weapons of War." Mental Hygiene.	158
SIMONEIT, Max. Wehrpsychologie	29
ALLPORT, Floyd H. and Simpson, Mary M. "Broadcasting to an Enemy Country: What Appeals Are Effective and Why." Journal of Social Psychology.	92
SLEEPER, Raymond S. "Air Power the Cold War, and Peace." Air University Quarterly Review.	162
SMITH, Chitra M. International Communication and Political Warfare - An Annotated Bibliography.	10
SPEIER, Hans. Social Order and the Risks of War: Papers in Political Sociology.	35
SPEIER, Hans. "Psychological Warfare Reconsidered." Rand Corp.	150

STANFORD UNIVERSITY. The Hoover Library and Institute.	11
STEED, Wickham. The Fifth Arm.	36
STORY, Dale. "Psywar in Korea." Combat Forces Journal.	129
SULLIVAN, John. Propaganda Handbook.	17
SUMMERS, Robert C. ed. America's Weapons of Psychological Warfare.	12
SUMMERS, Robert C. ed. America's Weapons of Psychological Warfare.	53
SUPREME HEADQUARTERS, ALLIED EXPEDITIONARY FORCE. Psychological Warfare Division, S.H.A.E.F.: An Account of its Operations in the Western European Campaigns, 1944-1945.	67
"TACTICAL PSYCHOLOGICAL WARFARE: THE COMBAT PSYCHOLOGICAL WARFARE DETACHMENT."	74
TAYLOR, Edmond. Strategy of Terror.	22
HANSI (Jean Jacques Waltz), and E. Tonnelat. "Across Enemy Lines." Divisional Interpreters of the Officers Reserve Corps, French Army.	24
"UNITED NATIONS COMMAND OPERATIONS IN KOREA." Dept. of State Bulletin.	98
U.S. ARMY. TWELFTH ARMY GROUP. History: Publicity and Psychological Warfare.	85
U.S. FIRST ARMY. Report of Operations, 23 February to 8 May 1945.	89
U.S. Dept of the Air Force. Psychological Warfare Program.	68
U.S. Dept. of the Air Force. Psychological Warfare in Norwegian Maneuvers.	86
U.S. DEPARTMENT OF THE ARMY. Psychological Warfare in Combat Operations. Field Manual FM-33-5.	75
U.S. Dept of the Army. GNA Propaganda Leaflets.	69
U.S. Dept of the Army. Research on Army Psychological Warfare Training.	79
U.S. DEPARTMENT OF STATE. Office of Intelligence Research. Strategic Aims of Axis vs. American Broadcasts.	83
U.S. FIFTH ARMY. Functions of the Fifth Army Combat Propaganda Team.	76
U.S. EIGHT ARMY. Report of the commanding General, 8th Army, on the Palwan and Zamboanga Operation, Victor III and IV.	88

U.S. STRATEGIC BOMBING SURVEY. MORALE DIVISION. The Effects of Bombing on German Morale.	65
U.S. Third Army. After Action Report, 1 August 1944- 9 May 1945	90
U.S. STRATEGIC BOMBING SURVEY. MORALE DIVISION: The Effects of Strategic Bombing on Japanese Morale.	66
U.S. WAR DEPARTMENT. What is Propaganda?	77
U.S. War Dept. General Staff. Syllabus of Psychological Warfare.	78
VATCHER, William H. Jr. Combat Propaganda: Okinawa Campaign.	84
SCHERKE, Feliz, and Vitzthum, Ursula. (Eds.). Bibliographie der Geistigen Kriegfuhrung.	8
WASHINGTON PUBLIC OPINION LABORATORY. Physical Characteristics of Leaflets: A Survey of the Literature.	70
WEAVER, Lt Col. John O. "Stock Number 56-C-13065-H." Military Review.	130
WHITE, Ralph K. "Hitler, Roosevelt, and the Nature of War Propaganda." Journal of Abnormal and Social Psychology.	151
WILMIT, Fred W. "The Infantry and Psychological Warfare." Infantry School Quarterly.	141
WOOLBERT, Robert Gale. Foreign Affairs Bibliography: A Selected and Annotated List of Books on International Relations 1932-1942.	13
YARNOLD, Kenneth. Fear in Battle.	81
"YOUR DEFENSE AGAINST ENEMY PROPAGANDA." Armed Forces Talk.	142
ZACHARIAS, Ellis M. Secret Missions: The Story of an Intelligence Officer.	64

www.ingramcontent.com/pod-product-compliance
Lightning Source LLC
Chambersburg PA
CBHW081917180426

43199CB00036B/2819